The Lightworker's Handbook
A Spiritual Guide to Eliminating Fear

Carole Gold

The Lightworker's Handbook
A Spiritual Guide to Eliminating Fear

Outskirts Press, Inc.
http://www.outskirtspress.com

ISBN: 978-1-4327-6890-4

PRINTED IN THE UNITED STATES OF AMERICA

Dedication

In appreciation and gratitude for my daughter, Zoe, whose Hebrew name is Zohar meaning Light. You are that in my life.

In appreciation and gratitude for the darkness, without which I never could have found The Light.

In appreciation and gratitude for all the brave Souls who volunteered for the position of Lightworker...even if you forgot you said "Yes." Awaken now and bask in the warmth and joy of The Light.

Preface

The Lightworker's Handbook brings much needed guidance as your Consciousness awakens in this new millennium. The world is going through a "realignment process" that causes the breakdown of previously existing patterns of behavior and resolution. This realignment can cause temporary confusion and yet, at the same time, seem strangely familiar and affirming. How two such contradictory perceptions can simultaneously co-exist is one of Life's paradoxes.

All of the book's content has been born from my personal experience. This is not to say that you should take my knowing as your own. Every teaching herein leads to one immutable conclusion: You are a unique and invaluable aspect of The God Source manifested in physical matter to achieve, through personal experience, your own knowing.

I, and all Lightworkers, delight in your individuality, glory in your awakening and patiently await your inevitable return to Oneness.

The Lightworker's Handbook

A Spiritual Guide to Eliminating Fear

The Lightworker's Creed
FEARLESS CHANGE

This book is a call to action.

If it's in your hand, consider that you have been called and in return you have answered. What you have been called *to* is the purpose for which you were born. This purpose is explained in the following pages. All that is asked is that you be fully conscious and receptive as you read. The rest will occur on its own.

Welcome home. It's good to be here with you.

If you have been following global events, or even if you haven't but simply take a look around you Now, what you see is a great deal of ineptitude, confusion and fear. Most efforts, whether economic, political or social, seem unable to affect much good or solve the problems we know need solving.

In fact, it looks increasingly as if we're in a downward spiral.

But to where?

No one seems to know for sure and the uncertainty is unnerving.

The cause of our current condition, depending upon your perspective, may be one or more of the following:

1. We in the West have been self-absorbed and greedy.

2. The world is overpopulated and cannot sustain its inhabitants.

3. Humans have disrespected the natural environment, and other life forms, thus creating a fatal imbalance.

4. Having disregarded our responsibility to the Earth, we have polluted the planet and destroyed the atmosphere with carbon emissions.

5. Certain individuals, religious or political groups intend to dominate the world using whatever means necessary to achieve their ends.

6. Capitalism is evil.

In seeking to cast blame, this list could go on indefinitely.

Regardless of which reason you think may be the *cause*, our inability to solve the many problems we face has birthed two schools of thought on what the overall solution might be.

These two schools of thought are:

1. God, or

2. A global government.

Which brings us to why you are reading this book.

Neither of these is the answer.

You are the answer.

You consciously chose to be born Now.

You consciously agreed to bring Light and clarity to a reality immersed in darkness and confusion that lost its bearings on the way home.

You consciously agreed to go unconscious until you could fulfill your intended purpose.

You have wandered, at times unconscious and at other times semi-conscious, throughout your entire life until recently when you began to fully move into Conscious Awareness of your true Self.

As you read these words you are thinking that this all sounds very "out there" and at the same time something within you is saying, "Yes!"

That *something* is Who You Are and why you are here.

You are not alone.

There is much work to be done Now and you cannot do it by yourself. You have your specific role to fulfill in the larger unfolding, but you are part of a Family of Lightworkers. You can easily recognize and connect with other Lightworkers once you fully embrace and acknowledge your purpose.

Allow your true identity to permeate your heart and mind. Begin Now.

A Lightworker recognizes fear and moves beyond it.

A Lightworker respects all life.

A Lightworker never stops growing.

A Lightworker is in search of Truth.

A Lightworker is passionate about what it knows to be true.

A Lightworker listens from within and without.

A Lightworker never stops trying to be better at unveiling the heart.

A Lightworker is indignant at encountering deceit.

A Lightworker weeps from both joy and suffering.

A Lightworker cannot tolerate unequal justice.

A Lightworker is a way-shower.

A Lightworker sees Light in everyone and everything.

A Lightworker inspires movement toward Oneness.

A Lightworker is a Light magnet.

This is how we find each other.

Spiritual Beings having a human experience are always in choice. We call this Free Will. As a Lightworker, it is helpful to understand the several paths set before you in order to choose wisely. Because there is much confusion about the way, it is important to be able to distinguish for yourself, as well as for others who seek you out, the path that leads to Oneness.

The Path of Restoration
This path leads to bringing back into existence, and reestablishing, a former or familiar condition.

A Lightworker does not take this path for it ends in the restoration or reestablishment of what worked in the past and disregards the unique qualities of Now.

The Path of Transformation

This path leads to changing the form, appearance, structure, nature and character of what is, so as to make it unrecognizable.

A Lightworker does not take this path because, absent wisdom and insight, it can result in the elimination of all that exists in the Now without distinguishing Light from darkness.

The Path of Transcendence

This path leads to rising above or beyond what is. It surpasses by elevation, extent, and degree.

This is the path of a Lightworker. It is taken *on purpose* to rise above what has been in order to experience All from a higher vantage point. From this elevated perspective, you can know what serves the Light and what does not.

The Path of Transcendence is the path of the Lightworker on the way to illumination and enlightenment for All.

Now is *not* time to return to some past paradigm, or to so transform our current existence as to make it unrecognizable. The time has come, *as have you*, to move to higher ground and elevate the frequency from which your consciousness perceives everything.

Your purpose is to shine Light upon an alternative and powerful way to heal the separation that has caused the problems facing Earth and its inhabitants.

This alternative way is The Path of Transcendence.

With this vision you, as a Lightworker, will assist all those seeking guidance in how to navigate new territory and accomplish what has been impossible to achieve on the journey home... until Now.

God exists.

However, It experiences Itself *in action* only through *You*.

God is not the solution.

You are.

You are a moving force that can open a portal to an alternate field where separation is unknown and Oneness is the norm. You will accomplish this as you move into full recognition of Who You Are and of what you are capable. The effect of this realization will be magnified exponentially once you align with other Lightworkers engaged in the same work.

This alignment is called co-creation.

Oneness is not a political solution. It is neither socialism nor a one-world government. It cannot be forced into being by manipulation, exploitation or legislation. Its vehicles of transmission are Love and Truth.

Oneness is an independent mind guided by a compassionate heart.

Its unified power creates worlds. Literally.

Love is the primary characteristic of Light.

If you add the "L" from "Love" to "Aloneness" you get AllOneness.

Love is what ends the illusion of separation.
In the Light of Love there is only One.

If you know these words to be true, not only in your mind but in the innermost core of your Being, it is time to act. Now.

That is why you have read this far.

You are a Lightworker fully employed in service to the Light.

An Electromagnetic Field (EMF) is the Light of Source that illuminates but does not consume. As a Lightworker, your mission and purpose is to correct the misunderstanding and misapplication of an EMF. An EMF improperly transmitted shows up as the following equation:

$$E+M=F$$

Exploitation + **M**anipulation = **F**ear

Fear is the misuse of electromagnetic energy that immobilizes whatever it encounters.

A Lightworker is the bearer of electromagnetic energy that enlightens and energizes.

Begin Now.

A Lightworker's Ten Guiding Principles

Live the truths you know in your heart to be life affirming.

Do not participate in behavior that perpetuates separation.

Pursue only that which you are passionate about.

Release all thoughts of lack and limitation.

Radiate abundance as it is your essence and birthright.

Refuse participation in deceit of any kind.

Assume responsibility for your every thought, word and deed.

Keep an eye and heart open for fellow Lightworkers.

Remember all the energy flowing through you emanates from Oneness.

Do with God's energy what you would have Oneness know.

We have each awakened Here and Now *on purpose.*

It's the appointment you scheduled and forgot about.

Remember Now.

There is only One of Us.

The English to Spirit Dictionary

The world was created through sound frequency.

In the beginning was the Word,
and the Word was with God,
and the Word was God.
John 1:1 - King James Bible

When Moses killed the Egyptian who
was beating the Hebrew slave,
Moses did so by reciting
the secret Name of God.
Shlomo Yitzchaki known as "Rashi,"
French rabbi and commentator 1040 –1105

A Lightworker knows the power of words.

Introduction

One of the responsibilities of a Lightworker is to assist others in understanding some of the basic concepts of the new paradigm. The careful use of language is critical in achieving this goal. However, it is first necessary that you remember the higher frequency usage of certain key words.

The following is an introduction to new paradigm vocabulary. When you become familiar with the meaning and usage of these words, you will be able to help others do the same. This vocabulary facilitates living in the higher frequencies of Light.

Depending upon your level of Consciousness and the amount of Light entering and emanating from you as you read these words, some of them will be instantly understandable while others may take some time to permeate old paradigm thinking. Be patient with yourself and others.

How we perceive and treat one another starts in the mind, moves through the heart and comes into physical form through words and deeds.

You've opened your mind.
You've opened your heart.
Now learn the words.
Then, practice the deeds.

Abundance

Definition: The infinite and eternal quantity of energy, or condition of existence, for all materiality and non-materiality alike.

Example: Sometimes I forget about abundance and think there's something important I could be lacking.

Adaptation

Definition: The mental and physical ability to respond with resilience to external stimuli and the intention to do so in conjunction with moving towards your higher Self.

Example: Adaptation is the key to surviving our rapidly-changing, technological world.

Agreement

Definition: Simultaneously vibrating at harmonious frequencies for a specific period of time for the highest mutual benefit of the parties.

Example: All relationships between people end by agreement.

Alignment

Definition: Harmony and mutual intention between, or among, two or more distinct frequencies.

Example: The results from a performance survey really helped the company bring several different departments into alignment.

Allow

Definition: To witness the opinions, actions or reactions of others without need to judge or realign them with one's own perspective.

Example: My friend and I are so different, but I enjoy spending time with her because she allows me to be me.

Anger

Definition: The convergence of ego, expectation, and impatience.

Example: The father would not have screamed at his children had he not felt anger over being bypassed for the promotion.

Atonement

Definition: The release of guilt, shame or regret combined with renunciation of any intention to recreate that which was released; always accompanied by feelings of peace, expansiveness and Love.

Example: Through atonement it is possible to begin anew.

Awareness

Definition: The alignment of one's consciousness with all physical and metaphysical activity occurring in the Now.

Example: The Rabbi's awareness of his congregant's suffering, over the loss of her child, caused him to sit and weep with her rather than try to speak with her.

Being

Definition (n): An individualized embodiment of Pure Consciousness.

Definition (v): Vibrating in the Now with neither memory nor projection of any thought mistakenly perceived as existing in "the past" or "the future."

Example: To say "I am being present" is redundant.

Certainty

Definition: The absence of doubt; the necessary foundation for making the manifestation of matter consistent with focused intention.

Example: My certainty that I would graduate law school eliminated every obstacle to that end.

Change

Definition: The natural process whereby Light energy moves from one configuration to another, creating temporary chaos as a byproduct.

Example: Change doesn't create stress; resistance to change does.

Chaos

Definition: The inexplicable or undetected intentional motion that occurs when a pattern is in process of being formed.

Example: Most teenagers between the ages of 12 and 17 experience chaos as they move into young adulthood.

Choice

Definition: An inherent characteristic of fragmented consciousness engaged in its own expansion and return toward Oneness; also known as "Free Will."

Example: I have made a choice not to engage in behavior with another that leaves me feeling less than peaceful within myself.

Compassion

Definition: Heart-based feeling for the physical and/or non-physical condition of another.

Example: Compassion is what connects one individual to another regardless of the physical distance in between.

Compromise

Definition: Ineffective or unsatisfactory quasi-resolution to conflict leading to further conflict at some indeterminate point in time.

Example: The Middle East is replete with compromise that has been a temporary solution to a continuous problem.

Co-Creation

Definition: The act of bringing forth and integrating mutually expressed wisdom contributions that result in an original and unforeseen outcome, surpassing the capacity of either contribution individually.

Example: The authoring of *Kali's Journey*, a spiritual book for children, was the result of co-creation with my friend.

Core

Definition: The bodily region known as the solar plexus corresponding to the metaphysical center of one's Soul knowledge, commonly referred to as intuition.

Example: When I come from my core I am able to think and act from inner guidance rather than external pressure.

Creativity

Definition: The process whereby an individual mirrors Source to bring about a unique expression of Self.

Example: I feel most energized when I am engaged in some form of creativity.

Darkness

Definition: A dense, static field manifesting emotionally as confusion and uncertainty, resulting from a restricted amount, or complete absence, of Light energy.

Example: When I am feeling lost or hopeless, meditation or prayer lifts the darkness.

Data

Definition: A quantity of Light received first through the spinal cord, then disseminated throughout the central nervous system for the purpose of regulating the function and performance of the physical body.

Example: Chiropractors realign the spine so that data can be optimally utilized.

Death

Definition: The process whereby the Consciousness contained within dense matter is released and continues to vibrate independently of it.

Example: At age 13, I saw my grandfather's body in a casket and turned to my father and said, "Now I know there is no such thing as death. That's not Grandpop, that's his 'suitcase.'"

Divine Feminine

Definition: A fundamental and essential aspect of Light characterized by receptivity that compliments and enhances the manifesting aspect of Light known as the masculine.

Example: For millennia, attempts have been made to diminish the Divine Feminine's role in co-creation.

Divine Timing

Definition: The orchestrated intersection of energies such that the outcome is of the highest frequency.

Example: Divine Timing in your life works like putting together a puzzle; a partial picture may unfold from the pieces you hold but the puzzle won't be complete until all the pieces, held by everyone concerned, are in their proper place.

Earth

Definition: An energetically calibrated location in time/space designed to maximize both the opportunity and the path to reunite with the Source of All energy.

Example: Earth experiences can be joyful or painful but never without the opportunity to move closer to Source.

Ego

Definition: A dense, lower vibration energy configured to maintain the illusion of separation by obstructing the reception of higher vibration energy transmissions.

Example: When someone has an opinion you perceive as different and in opposition to yours, it's your ego that makes you angry when you can't convince them to see it your way.

Emotion

Definition: An internal and behavioral indicator of the degree to which an individual is aligned with Love or fear.

Example: His display of emotion was hurtful.

Energy

Definition: A quantum of Light that emanates from Source which provides the vehicle for manifesting Pure Consciousness into matter.

Example: The amount of focused energy I give to reaching my goal is the best determining factor of my likelihood of success.

Expectation

Definition: An intention tied to a particular outcome lacking trust in co-creation.

Example: Expectation of others does not allow for their Free Will.

Experience

Definition: A direct personal encounter with a thing, thought, situation or other; the only basis for knowing with certainty.

Example: It is through experience that I know miracles occur.

Faith

Definition: The state of trust prior to knowing.

Example: I had faith that I would make a good lawyer.

Fear

Definition: An emotional frequency designed to bring you present in a life-threatening situation, causing irrational and reactive behavior if retained once the threat is removed.

Example: The fear of dogs stayed with her throughout her life because she had been attacked as a child.

Forgiveness

Definition: A spiritual, heart-centered state of being that heals oneself, others and relationships while simultaneously negating all prior acts not originating in Love.

Example: Forgiveness of Self and others is a necessary step on the way to Oneness.

Free Will

Definition: The mechanism by which an individual can choose to move toward or away from union with The Light.

Example: Showing either compassion or contempt is an exercise of Free Will.

Frequency

Definition: One of many possible wavelengths at which an individual receives, perceives and transmits data.

Example: Sometimes the frequency on which I know something cannot be seen or heard outside my heart.

Giving

Definition: The voluntary release of heart-based energy with the intention to elevate the frequency of another.

Example: At age 12, my daughter's insistence on giving her birthday money to a homeless person was a lesson to everyone present.

Gratitude

Definition: The expression of an acute awareness for the gift of life.

Example: Gratitude is the way to acknowledge Source daily.

Healer

Definition: One who is able to align their heart with the heart of another, in perfect attunement with Source, thereby restoring equilibrium.

Example: When the healer touched me, tears of joy came from the release of pain.

Heart

Definition: A filtering system that moves all Light data throughout the body and is capable of holding the highest frequency of Light known as Love.

Example: The heart is our internal GPS...God Positioning System.

Honesty

Definition: Observation and communication absent any agenda; the knowing and sharing of what Is.

Example: It is not possible to sustain a co-creative relationship without honesty.

Impatience

Definition: The absence of trust in Divine Timing manifested as a need to control outcomes.

Example: Impatience always ends in being at the wrong place at the wrong time.

Intend

Definition: To direct concentrated thought energy toward a particular manifestation.

Example: When I started law school at age thirty-three I told everyone, "I intend to graduate."

Intuit

Definition: To access information transmitted on a frequency beyond three dimensional reality and outside of time.

Example: A psychic intuits information.

Joy

Definition: A feeling and spiritual state of Being unaffected by external occurrences and predicated upon acceptance of what Is.

Example: I can be filled with joy on a dreary, cloudy day when nothing I've planned works out.

Judgment

Definition: The primary means of separation.

Example: The judgment I make about you is a measurement of my distance from Source.

Kindness

Definition: A spontaneous act emanating from alignment with Oneness that elevates the frequency of all involved.

Example: The kindness I share is the Love I receive.

Know

Definition: To have certainty as a result of direct experience.

Example: I know my ability with words.

Light

Definition: The Source of All That Is being the highest frequency in which energy can transmit Itself.

Example: Bringing Light into matter elevates its frequency.

Love

Definition: A fundamental property of Light, the other being Truth.

Example: I love you is Self love.

Loss

Definition: The illusion, emanating from fragmented consciousness, that a temporary absence is permanent.

Example: Job loss is nothing more than career change.

Manifest

Definition: To bring into existence that which is conceptually and consciously intended.

Example: When enough humans manifest Love, harmony and peace will be the norm.

Meditation

Definition: A vehicle for taking the journey within.

Example: Since I began meditation, I am more peaceful and able to know more of Source.

Nature

Definition: Living art.

Example: For me, all of the answers to life can be discerned within Nature.

Now

Definition: The eternal moment of creation.

Example: Past and future are misperceptions of Now.

Oneness

Definition: Undifferentiated Source of All That Is.

Example: I suspect the word "holy" derived its meaning from the concept of "wholeness" or Oneness.

Opportunity
Definition: The positive interpretation of a problem, obstacle or detour.

Example: An opportunity to grow spiritually presents itself every day.

Paradigm Shift
Definition: An expansion of the boundaries and capacity of Consciousness while within matter.

Example: The rapid change taking place in societal and governmental structures is the result of a paradigm shift.

Passion
Definition: The quantum of emotion that, when combined with intention, directly and proportionately affects matter.

Example: When my passion is subdued, my writing is less inspiring.

Pattern

Definition: An energetic repetition that, when manifested as behavior, supports or impedes growth.

Example: Busting negative patterns has become my favorite pastime.

Patience

Definition: Acceptance of Self plus the allowing of others.

Example: My lack of patience was a way to avoid being in the Now.

Peace

Definition: The experience of absolute stillness within silence.

Example: In peace you feel your connection with everyone and everything.

Power

Definition: The result of knowing your essence is love, your intention creates your experience, and your strongest desire is to be One.

Example: To live life in your own power is All There Is.

Purpose

Definition: An individualized contribution toward Oneness.

Example: Discovering your purpose is a celebration along the journey within.

Question

Definition: A tool used to excavate knowing.

Example: We only question what we have not personally experienced.

Reality

Definition: A multi-faceted, holographic matrix selectively and subjectively experienced.

Example: My reality and I are ever-changing.

Receive

Definition: To accept the inflow of energy absent judgment.

Example: While love may be expressed in many ways, only an open heart can receive it.

Release
Definition: To honor and allow energy a change in direction.

Example: It was painful to release my husband and me from our marriage.

Remember
Definition: To reunite with dispersed energy.

Example: I remember that it's possible to manifest what I visualize and focus upon.

Separate
Definition: A misperception of the relationship of fragmented energy to Itself.

Example: I cannot know Oneness if I think I am separate from You.

Silence
Definition: The sound of peace found within stillness.

Example: In meditative silence I am not distracted by my thoughts.

Source
Definition: Undifferentiated Oneness.

Example: All matter, in the form of energy, flows continually to and from Source.

Spirituality
Definition: Heart-centered awareness aligned with Oneness manifested through thought and action.

Example: When I fully opened to spirituality, I felt on purpose for the first time in my life.

Steward
Definition: A position of personal responsibility in caring for and managing the resources of the physical world.

Example: While it is possible to *legally* purchase real estate, from a spiritual perspective, one becomes not a property owner but a property steward.

Surrender

Definition: Acceptance of the Now and relinquishment of the outcome.

Example: When you surrender to what you cannot seem to control, it becomes easier to be joyful.

Time

Definition: A construct for managing physical reality at a specific level of Consciousness.

Example: As our Consciousness awakens and expands, the paradigm of time collapses.

Thought

Definition: The inception point for manifesting, in matter, that which is non-material.

Example: I began to heal when I replaced the thought that I was sick with the thought that I was well.

Transcend

Definition: To move beyond a limited perception into one with a more expansive boundary and higher vibratory rate.

Example: Our society needs to transcend how we perceive and experience change.

Truth

Definition: The symphony of elements that support Light and all life.

Example: Truth is spiritually empowering.

Trust

Definition: An aspect of faith that precedes certainty.

Example: I need trust only that which I have not experienced.

Us

Definition: A simulation of Oneness that results in temporary unity but implies an underlying belief in separation.

Example: Once you experience Oneness, you know there is only One of Us.

Visualize

Definition: To focus on a thought with certainty and the intention to manifest it.

Example: I visualized graduating law school before I knew that I could.

Wisdom

Definition: Known aspects of Oneness that are of beneficial value to all Conscious Beings.

Example: Moving along a spiritual path has given me wisdom that changes how I perceive myself in relationship to humanity.

Within

Definition: The path of fragmented Consciousness in returning to Itself.

Example: I've traveled the world but it turns out the only journey worth taking was the journey within.

You

Definition: The object of differentiation caused by unawakened Consciousness.

Example: When I am in That Place in me, and You are in That Place in You, there is only One of Us.

Now

You have awakened.

It excites the mind and quickens the heart to have come this far. Move forward, in unison, to complete *our* work with renewed understanding of *your* true essence. You have known both Oneness and separation. Now, through conscious choice, you return once again to Oneness. It has always been both the journey and the destination, for All Is One.

Acknowledgements

To Craig Rentmeester, of Relevante Marketing, for the book's interior formatting, graphics placement, cover design and an abundance of constructive suggestions along the way. Craig walked the distance on the book's development and made the journey more enjoyable for me because of it.

To Jack Saady, of Jack Saady Photography, for my cover photo. Jack sees the Light within and captures it on film.

To Katharine Menton, my spiritual mentor, who never fails to elevate the discourse. Katharine planted the seed that grew into "The English to Spirit Dictionary."

To Hilary Green, dear friend, sister traveler and Master of grace under pressure who was the first to read the manuscript and said, "Perfect." Knowing her love of essential truth, I was encouraged onward.

Finally, to Dr. Marlene Kenion, who sees only the highest good in each of us. She's the absolute best mirror to look into on those days when we forget.

About the Author

CAROLE GOLD is a Lightworker who gave up a successful law practice in 2001 to follow her truth. As an inspirational speaker, motivational coach, intuitive and mediator her mission is to inspire and guide others in discovering and living their own truth. Carole's blog, Gold Post-It, offers spiritual insights into the highest lessons we can take from everyday occurrences at home and around the globe. Her co-authored children's book, *Kali's Journey*, will teach children spiritual laws of the Universe in easy-to-understand terms. Her honesty and willingness to share her personal journey make for compelling presentations on fear, change, ethics, mission, purpose, intuition, stress, and relationships. Carole is focused on guiding other Lightworkers in leading the way to eliminate the fear, resistance and stress that keep us from spiritual growth.

Email: Contact@CaroleGold.com
Website: www.CaroleGold.com

Breinigsville, PA USA
01 April 2011
258988BV00001B/2/P